Introduction

Do you want to learn the secrets to effectively managing your remote employees?

If you have always wanted to make a positive difference in the lives of your remote team members while helping them, yourself, and your company achieve monumental success, then this book and the secrets you will learn within is for you!

Aren't the days of working remote going away?

There have been numerous high-profile companies that have terminated the practice of allowing their employees to work remotely for a number of reasons. However, there are even more companies that are discovering the value of being able to hire the best employees regardless of their physical location to their offices.[1]

For managers or would-be managers of this remote workforce, the task to lead and serve your employees can be overwhelming and downright confusing with all the opinions that are floating around in the blogosphere (Yes, that is a word).

Why should I read this book? Aren't there already a number of management books that discuss the remote workforce?

This is not a book that discusses the benefits or downsides of a remote workforce, there are numerous books, blogs, and opinions that you can gather related to that topic.

This is a book that pulls back the curtains and provides the secrets to managing your remote employees (and possibly even your non-remote employees as well).

Is it necessary to read this entire book?

I would highly recommend you read the book. My goal is for you to be successful in managing your remote employees and taking an hour or so to read through this book will pay back that time tenfold. I am that confident that these secrets will make you a better manager and employee.

Remember *PRETAIM*.

- **Purpose**: Have a common purpose to rally your team around.

- **Relationships**: Purposely develop and encourage positive working relationships through communication with your team members and among your team members.

- **Encourage success**: Develop a means to help your team be successful beyond just the tasks they have been assigned to complete.

- **Tools**: Provide and use the best tools to allow your teams to be successful.

- **Availability**: Make yourself available to your team.

- **Instill trust**: Ask your team to trust you and then live up to that trust.

- **Manage beyond**: Your focus should be on serving your team, not yourself.

Why should I listen to you?

In the event that you are prepared to dive right in and learn the secrets to managing remote employees, feel free to ignore this section and skip to the <u>next chapter</u>. For those of you that want to take a little time in getting to know me, here is a brief synopsis of my experience (including both successes and failures) over the last 30 years.

FLYING HIGH WITH THE UNITED STATES AIR FORCE

Black boxes

At the age of seventeen, I joined the United States Air Force and began my service in the New York Air National Guard stationed in Hancock Field in Syracuse, New York. I was trained to be an avionics technician, supporting an F-16 Squadron.

My job was to receive *black boxes*[2] that were removed from the airplanes by flight line mechanics who had diagnosed the box as not working properly.

The flight line mechanics were able to diagnose the location of the failure. It was their job to replace the black box with a working box and send the failed box to my team to open it up and repair the inner workings.

Communication, the secret of all secrets
This is where I learned one of my first secrets in managing remote employees: Communication.

The flight line mechanic is told by the pilot that there was a problem that he discovered while either inspecting the plane for flight or during a flight.

The flight line mechanic will ask questions to perform their own diagnosis of where the problem might be and perform their tests to determine the point of failure.

Once the mechanic determines the point of failure, and if the failure is associated with one of these boxes, they will replace it and send the failed box to my team.

What we have here is a failure to communicate
Do you see where communication is important in the above steps? The avionics technicians have not had a chance to talk to the pilots directly, so they have to collect their information from the flight line mechanic.

If the flight line mechanic cannot provide enough information, then the avionics technician may be flying blind (pun intended) in diagnosing the actual problem.

Ensuring proper, timely, and accurate communication is important for every employee (regardless of position).

Getting up in the air
Years later I transferred to Peterson Air Force Base in Colorado Springs, Colorado and was trained to work as a crew chief on C-130 Cargo Aircrafts. In this role, I was called to support our troops in Desert Shield/Storm.

The aircraft I supported and other aircrafts from my unit were called to Incirlik Air Base in Adana, Turkey. We were called to support the *Operation Provide Comfort* [3] military operation that was responsible for defending the Kurdish refugees who had fled their homes in Northern Iraq and were perilously located between the Iraqi military and the Turkish border.

The aircraft I supported was one of the first planes to provide relief items that were crucial to the survival of the thousands of people who had left their homes with nothing more than the clothes on their backs.

Common purpose

Even though I supported multiple operations during my time in the military, this particular operation showed me the importance of having a common purpose as a team (The P in *PRETAIM*).

All of my fellow airman and I were committed to providing the tools necessary for these Kurdish Refugees to survive under very difficult conditions. This commitment did not waiver even when we were faced with danger from the Iraqi military and the Kurdish defenders who inadvertently shot at our planes thinking that we were part of the Iraqi military.

As you can expect, this ended abruptly once we started dropping supplies. However, the feeling of accomplishment and pride at working together to help these refugees reinforced the importance of everyone having a common purpose and working toward the goals to achieve that purpose.

Son, you are grounded

Once I returned to my home base in Colorado, I was pulled aside by my Chief and thanked for all the hard work while deployed to the Middle East. However, he had determined that I was not the best crew chief in his unit.

As a bonus, he noted that I had a wonderful personality and desire to help others. Even though this sounds like I was being dropped by a girlfriend, it was the best thing that ever happened to me and changed my life forever.

A star is born

My Chief reassigned me to an On the Job Training office to help others get trained and qualified to perform their duties in the unit. Here is where I found my passion for training others and helping people achieve success.

I stayed in that position for a few years and then transferred to a Base Education office where I was able to support a larger number of airmen find success in their careers.

In the Base Education office, I was also called upon to support a small computer and network office that was introducing networked personal computers to the organization.

I was able to combine my passion for technology and helping others into a role of training end users on how to perform their jobs using this new technology. A career was born.

IT'S A WONDERFUL CIVILIAN LIFE

Time to move on
After approximately 8 years of service, I left the military and moved on to working at Colorado Springs Utility in Colorado Springs as a technical trainer helping employees learn Microsoft Windows and Office, Lotus Notes, and other applications to support the growth of technology in an effort to modernize the workforce.

Here is where I really grew in my understanding of curriculum development and delivery of technology to a wide range of audiences.

Being available
This is also where I learned the value of making myself available (the A in *PRETAIM*) to my customers. I developed the practice of open office hours where I could help any of my customers during defined hours with any project on which they were working.

I was able to assist my customers with such things writing formulas in Microsoft Excel, to creating databases in Microsoft Access, to dabbling in this "new" thing called HTML to create web pages.

Stepping deeper into technology
Within a few years, now finding success in civilian life, I decided to move on to more challenging opportunities in technology and technical training.

I took a position with a company called Avanti that developed Electronic Design Automation software to help companies use our tools to develop the next generation integrated circuits (or chips) that are used in almost every piece of modern electronic devices.

Thinking outside the classroom
Helping to train engineers in the use of our software stretched me in my understanding of technology, and it showed me new ways we could train our end users. This brought me to the idea of using the web to deliver our training. Unfortunately, we had a very limited budget to make that happen.

Most companies were still using computer-based training on CDs to deliver their training — the idea of a web-based learning management system (LMS) was still in its infancy stages.

Let's get ready to program
I decided to dig into the Perl programming language, using the Common Gateway Interface module to create my own LMS.

With a limited budget, I also took advantage of using an open-source database called MySQL as the means to store the data that was necessary to deliver our training. I also used MySQL to track and monitor which customers were taking our courses.

This led me to some great successes, but it also led to some of the most difficult relationships with my fellow employees.

Instill trust, live up to that trust
Years later, Avanti was acquired by Synopsys and things changed for me. My manager had left the company prior to the acquisition and for months my team and I were without direct management. The director of training at Synopsys asked me to take on the role of online learning manager once the acquisition was final.

My Avanti peers would now be reporting directly to me along with a few employees from Synopsys. Here is where another secret was learned and lived out: Instilling trust (the I in *PRETAIM*).

For the next year and a half, I worked with each of my employees and my management and found more successes than failures in learning to manage remote employees.

A mentor was found, but the world had changed

My director was phenomenal and mentored me to great success in improving my understanding of technical training and management, but the idea of applying management techniques to remote employees was still in its infancy, and I struggled to develop a unified team.

Eventually, the dot com bubble busted in 2003 and the majority of the training division (including myself and my team) were laid off.

Time to take a break

After being laid off in late 2003, I decided to take a break from technical training and my profession and returned to school to study non-technical education skills for what I thought was a change in my chosen career path.

I was wrong, but the two years that I spent studying and growing in what I thought was going to become a new profession were some of the most valuable years for me and my family.

Called back in to action

In late 2005, I received a call from the new director of training for the company MySQL AB. He was creating a new division that was going to be responsible for developing curriculum and delivering training on the open-source MySQL database.

With my experience with MySQL, curriculum development, technical training, and courseware delivery, he felt I would be a great addition to his newly developed team. The offer was too good to pass up, and I found myself back in the technical training world again.

The shining star in the world of the remote workforce
MySQL AB was primarily made up of remote workers from all corners of the world, and I jumped back into the remote workforce with a passion.

I found myself in a dream come true and the management of MySQL AB was phenomenal, and there seemed to be no stopping what we could accomplish as an organization.

Relationships are key
MySQL ABs success led to some very interested buyers (including Sun Microsystems and Oracle). Sun Microsystems won out and MySQL AB was purchased for 1 billion dollars in 2008.

Two years later in 2010, Oracle purchased Sun Microsystems along with its technologies, including MySQL.

The transition from Sun Microsystems, and then to Oracle, saw the majority of MySQL ABs original management and a large number of the original employees move on to other adventures.

I moved on myself in 2011, but not before learning another secret managing remote employees: Relationships are important. (the R in *PRETAIM*)

Use the tools available
In 2011, I took a position with Message Systems, Inc. as a technical trainer supporting their mail transport agent software. Message Systems software was being used at the time by the big names in social media to manage and deliver email to their customers.

I would have to admit that I thought sending email was easy, but when you are sending millions upon millions of emails an hour, things get very complicated.

Message Systems was a leader in the space and again I learned a completely new technology and was able to train engineers on how to set up and use this leading-edge technology.

In this position, I was eventually promoted to Director of Training and learned another secret to managing remote employees: Use technology to keep the lines of communication open (the T in *PRETAIM*).

Know your competencies
In 2014, I decided to move on to a training delivery company called Maverick Solutions, LLC that was located within minutes of my home. Maverick Solutions was the leading competitor in the Oracle training space.

I had known the leadership of Maverick Solutions for years through my church and when there was a need for them to have a true curriculum development team, I was offered the privilege to develop the team and the program as their director of curriculum development.

In this role, I worked in the corporate headquarters office in Wake Forest, North Carolina, but a number of my employees and other staff members that I interacted with were remote.

I had the great opportunity to learn from my leadership on the importance of supporting and living out what you believe and having it affect the culture of your company. This is another secret to managing remote employees; aligning yourself and evaluating yourself against the company's set competencies, enabling your employees for success (the E in *PRETAIM*).

Maverick Solutions was acquired by GP Strategies in 2016 and continues to be a leader in the Oracle training space.[4]

A book is born
That same year, after developing and growing an extremely successful curriculum development team, I moved on to a Canadian-based company called Pethealth Inc., supporting software products used by animal shelters and rescues to manage their animal populations. In my position as the technical training and engagement manager, I was able to truly define and live out the secrets of managing a remote workforce. My employees were spread out throughout the country, each individually working from their homes. It was in this outstanding environment where this book was born. A big thanks to the leadership of Pethealth Inc. for pushing me to share my knowledge internally.

Ready for another thirty years

That is my background as of the publication of this book. Thirty years summed up in a few pages was quite an exercise in being precise and to the point. However, please understand there were numerous challenges, struggles, and successes along the way that shaped the content of this book, and, I hope, shaped the lives of the men and women I had the pleasure of working alongside and serving throughout my career.

It is the people we get to share our lives with that shape who we are and how we are measured. I pray that my legacy is one of successes in this area of importance over any other area we could be measured by. I pray the same for you as well.

[1] http://globalworkplaceanalytics.com/telecommuting-statistics
[2] https://en.wikipedia.org/wiki/Black_box
[3] https://www.globalsecurity.org/military/ops/provide_comfort.htm
[4] http://www.mavericksolutions.net/about-us/

Secret One: Purpose

"When you're surrounded by people who share a passionate commitment around a common purpose, anything is possible" - Howard Schultz, Chairman & CEO, Starbucks

Remote teams, like all teams, want to be connected to something bigger than themselves. Providing them a purpose as a team allows them to connect individually with the purpose and see their part in the outcomes of that purpose.

How do I define my team's purpose in words?

Many companies have a mission statement for their overarching purpose to explain and define who they are and what is important to them. This is where you should start with the purpose statement for your own team. Here are some examples of company mission statements:

- "To help individuals and businesses realize their full potential." Microsoft

- "To organize the world's information and make it universally accessible and useful." Google

- "To spread the power of optimism." Life is Good

- "To build the best product, cause no unnecessary harm, use business to inspire and implement solutions to the environmental crisis." Patagonia

- "To create a better everyday life for the many people." IKEA

Mission Statement or Vision statement?
A mission statement defines who the company is, what they believe, and why they exist. Vision statements are developed from the mission statements and define where the company wants to be in the future. A large number of companies are bypassing the distinctiveness of two separate statements and creating one statement that includes both purposes.

I recommend that you take a moment to put your company's mission statement or vision statement in front of you. Once you have done so, let's connect your team's purpose statement to the company's statements.

> "The business is guided by a deep understanding of the needs and challenges facing animal welfare and our shared goal to build a stronger, safer global community for people and their pets." Pethealth, Inc. company mission statement

How do I connect my team's purpose to the company's purpose?

As the engagement services manager for the Pethealth software[5] products that are used by animal shelters and rescue groups, my team was responsible for training, implementing, and providing consulting services to the end users of the software. In this capacity, we were able to connect our team's purpose statement with the company's mission statement:

> *"To provide our software clients with the knowledge necessary to use our products in the most efficient manner for their organization and the processes they have implemented* to build a stronger, safer global community for people and their pets."- Pethealth Inc. Engagement Services team mission statement

We were able to connect the company's overarching purpose of providing a safe environment for pets and their owners to the software that was used day-in and day-out in the shelters and rescues that we were supporting.

We attempted to test every decision that we made against this purpose statement and the financial needs of the organization to ensure that our clients were receiving the best from us and would continue to receive the best from us in the years to come.

How do I connect my team members' individual responsibilities to the team's purpose?

Once you define your team's purpose, you can start to connect each individual team member's tasks to this purpose. You can accomplish this through the development of success factors for each employee.

The term "success factors" is associated with quantifying and tracking the performance of your employees in relation to your purpose and any associated Key Performance Indicators that you are using to evaluate how your organization is achieving its goals and objectives.

My team's success factors revolved around the following metrics:

- Client satisfaction scores that were obtained through surveys at the completion of training or consulting services.

    o This success factor connected with the "knowledge necessary to use our products in the most efficient manner" component of our team's purpose statement. If the clients were not learning from our training or not finding value in our consulting services, then we were failing in our purpose.

- Percentage of overall time spent in performing training or consulting services.

    o This success factor ensured that we were applying our time properly in meeting the needs of the client. If the majority of our time was spent talking internally about how we could meet the needs of our clients with very little time spent on actually meeting the needs of our clients, then again, we were failing in our purpose.

- The time that it took to develop and deliver training to our clients.

    o This success factor ensured that we were providing our clients with training and consulting products that were timely and relative to the tasks they were being asked to perform now or in the near future. If the development of our training or supporting aids were painstakingly slow to complete and make available to the clients, then our clients were not receiving the support they needed at the time they needed it, and we were failing in our purpose.

There were other, more specific success factors created that addressed the specific role and level that each individual was in, but each success factor had components of the success factors listed.

The success factors were evaluated monthly with each employee so that they understood exactly where they were with their performance in relation to the success factors they were being evaluated against.

You may find that remote employees gravitate as much, if not more, to the team's purpose and their individual success factors because their day-to-day tasks may be limited in seeing the outcome of their work on a regular basis.

Implementing this one secret will provide your remote employees with the sense of belonging and purpose that they may not feel otherwise since they are separated from the physical presence of you and other employees.

[5] http://www.pethealthinc.com/Our-Brands/PetPoint

Secret Two: Relationships

"Coming together is a beginning; keeping together is progress; working together is success." - Henry Ford

As employees, we spend our waking hours interacting more with our co-workers than with our spouses and families. This is true of both of on-premise employees and remote employees. With on-premise employees, a large percentage of the interactions are initiated by the employees themselves and are informal and face-to-face. These informal interactions provide on-premise employees the means to develop positive working relationships.

For remote employees, the process of developing positive working relationships must be initiated and maintained by their manager. This does not mean that individual remote employees are prevented or discouraged from developing positive working relationships on their own, but it does mean that managers cannot expect individual remote employees to do this naturally.

Why are good relationships in the workplace important? According to Kate McFarlin, in a *Houston Chronicle* article titled "Importance of Relationships in the Workplace,"[6] the benefits of fostering good relationships in the workplace include improved teamwork, improved employee morale, higher employee retention rate, and increased productivity.

How can I initiate and manage the process of developing positive working relationships among my remote team members?

One word: *Meetings.* Okay there's the secret, meetings. I know what you are thinking: "Really? *Another* meeting?"

I agree that the level of meetings in organizations can be overwhelming and have a large impact on the overall hours that an employee can actually perform the tasks they were hired to perform. So rather than thinking about another meeting, think about reinventing your existing meetings.

Before we talk about reinventing meetings, let's talk about the meetings that every manager should be having with their employees and then we will break down each meeting and share some secrets to reinvent the meetings to be more productive.

The two meetings that every manager should be having with their remote employees are:

1) Team Meetings
2) One-on-One Meetings

Team Meetings

The frequency of length of team meetings is dependent on the tasks that the teams are responsible for, but the secret is not to have too few or too many. My recommendations are no more than four a week, and no less than two a week. Meetings should be no more than one hour.

Once you determine the frequency and length of team meetings, the next step is to determine how they should be run.

Reinventing Meetings

Here is my secret to running effective team meetings while managing the development of positive relationships:

1) **Individual employees provide updates prior to the meeting.** Have your team members enter their updates since the last meeting in a tool that you use to communicate with each other as a team.

   These updates should be brief enough to provide context to what they have completed since they attended the last team meeting and include any impediments they are facing to be able to complete their tasks.

   Big Picture
   These updates are designed to give the entire team a big picture of what they are working on and the impediments they are facing.

   It is highly likely that if one employee is facing an impediment, the other employees may be facing the same impediment or will most likely face that impediment in the near future.

Where Work Happens

Slack (https://slack.com/) is the tool that I have used with my teams in the past to have them provide their updates. Slack's motto is "Where work happens" and I have found this tool to be extremely friendly and useful as a communication tool. However, it is not the only communication tool I have used in the past. We will discuss tools in a later chapter, but I will provide brief introductions to the tools throughout all the chapters.

2) **The first five minutes of the meeting is water cooler talk time.** The first five minutes of a meeting are designed to allow team members to have a quick break from one meeting to the next, a time to read the updates of the team, and a time to get caught up in each other's lives.

Natural Water Cooler Talk
At first, you may find yourself as the manager having to start the water cooler talk, but as the team becomes more comfortable with each other, this water cooler talk time will become natural and you will have to start to curb the conversations to fit within the five-minute time period.

However, if the five minutes turns into 10 minutes on a non-frequent regularity, I have allowed the conversations to span past the five minutes on occasions.

No need to shut down a good team-building conversation right at the five-minute mark if a few extra minutes would help wrap the conversation up properly.

3) **The manager presents items that have an impact on the entire team.** After the water cooler talk was finished, I would present the topics of note that had an effect on the whole team.

This is a good time to follow up on items that the whole team was responsible for completing, such as:

a) Friendly HR mandatory training reminders (without pointing out those who have not completed the training).

b) Updates you may want to pass on from management meetings that you have attended.

c) Any other topics that are important to the majority of the team.

4) **Individuals take turns interacting with the team.** This is where many meetings fail and where step 1 is going to be the secret to your reinventing your meetings.

When the individual is called upon to share in a team meeting, they do not have to say anything, because they have already stated what they were working on in the communication tool in step 1.

They do not have to rehash what they have been working on. They can simply say "no impediments", and we can move on to the next team member.

Working Together
This is also a time where fellow team members can ask the presenter questions about their updates, if further information is needed to support their needs, or to provide assistance.

In addition, you can learn more about their impediments and possibly discuss solutions with the team right then, or an action item can be set for the next meeting to come back and address.

Giving Back Time
This secret is going to change the way you run team meetings and give you back time in your day. Meaning, you no longer will have to listen to team members explain in detail what they have accomplished since the last meeting, since that is all written down in a historical record.

Who should go first taking turns?

The secret is birthdays. Deep down everybody wants the day of their birth to be recognized. Why not make it a big deal in every meeting by starting with the person who has the next birthday coming up? Then after the person with the next birthday coming up goes, the next birthday boy or girl goes, and so on.

As we get closer and closer to someone's birthday, the excitement of the birthday boy or girl is being raised and the team will naturally recognize them—making the process feel less forced.

If you want to shake things up a bit, every other week, go backwards and choose the person who last had a birthday, and then the person before that birthday, and so on.

I found my teams really appreciated that if their birthday was next on the list, they did not have to be the one always going first, especially if there were large gaps between birthdays.

---

5) **Topic of the day.** After the team has gone through their updates, you may want to have a regular topic discussed on a particular day. For example, in one company I was working for, we were responsible for professional services and making money.

Money Mondays

For one of my past employers, Mondays were *Money Mondays.* On Mondays, we would spend time in our meetings to discuss where we were at in presales conversations, current active services, services that were about to expire, assistance that was needed to complete a service that was falling behind, etc.

Training Tuesdays

Tuesdays were *Training Tuesdays* where each of us would take time providing some type of training to the rest of the team. Having folks assigned to teach on a particular topic on a particular day allowed for each team member to grow in their ability to present information, and it allowed the entire team to appreciate the challenges that were faced when presenting to the team.

Webinar Wednesdays

Wednesdays were *Webinar Wednesdays* where we discussed future training webinars we wanted to run or planned to run in the future. Lots of brainstorming took place here and lots of collaboration—another great tool to help develop positive relationships.

Survey Thursdays

Thursdays were *Survey Thursdays*, and we would use this time to discuss the feedback we were receiving from clients. We also looked-for ways to collect new feedback from clients and to find ways to encourage more feedback.

Free Fridays

Fridays were *Free Fridays*, and we would not meet. This allowed team members to have the time blocked off in their calendars to focus on growing themselves professionally or personally. I still asked the team to submit their updates in the communication tool, but we would interact through that tool versus actually having a meeting.

Keep it Positive

Team meetings must stay positive and focused on what the team can control. It is a very common practice to address problems in team meetings that lead to blaming others for the problems that are being encountered.

This blaming usually does not get directed to anyone on the call, but to those that are not on the calls (other teams, management above you, clients, etc.). This cannot be allowed and must be turned to what the team can control.

If there truly is a problem that cannot be controlled by the team, it is your responsibility as the manager to identify the problem and address the potential problem with the other team's manager, or your management, depending on your organization's autonomy and reporting structure.

If there is a problem that one team member needs to bring up that affects another team member, those problems must be addressed during one-on-one meetings. This is when the employee can bring up the problem to you.

During the one-on-one meetings, you and your employee can discuss the problem in detail, and if there is a need to bring it up in the team meeting, then you can work together on the delivery of the problem. This will ensure that the problem is presented in such a way that the other party is not seen in a negative light.

6) **End the meeting with your signature line.** I actually borrowed my signature line from a former manager I worked for (if you are reading this, you know who you are). My signature line was "go forth and be awesome". We were known as the A-Team (Awesome Team) because of this line, and it really was a great way to end our meetings.

This may sound corny to you, but I am telling you that this is a little-known secret to helping build positive relationships—being a little corny makes you more human and provides your team a level of comfort that they can be human, too.

One-on-One Meetings

The frequency and length of one-on-one meetings is dependent on the work that is being accomplished and the relationship needs between you and your employee.

Early on, you may find that meeting weekly for an hour is necessary to build trust and rapport with your employees, while later on, every other week for 30 minutes is all that is necessary.

Once you determine the frequency and length of one-on-one meetings, the next step is to determine how to run them. Here is my secret to running effective one-on-one meetings while managing the development of positive relationships:

It is not your meeting, it is your employee's meeting.
This is one of the most important concepts you can take away from this section and this book: one-on-one meetings with your employees should be led by the employee and the items the employee wants to talk about should be the priority.

If there is time after the employee has addressed all their needs from you, then you can bring up topics that you want to discuss. However, if the meeting time comes to an end and you still have topics you need to address with your employee, schedule another time to meet.

Review Success Factors
At least once a month, you should set aside time during the one-on-one meetings to discuss the current success factors and how the employee is performing against these metrics on a month to month basis.

It is not fair or respectful to only address the performance of an employee at annual review time without giving them the opportunity to see where they are at on a regular basis.

By reviewing an employee's performance against set success factors monthly, there are no surprises at the annual review time, and if there is a need to address performance issues, it is easier to address them earlier than later.

Review Company Set Competencies
Every company has a list of competencies they expect their employees to follow. If your company does not have a list of defined competencies, the next chapter will provide you with one of the best company set competencies I have had the pleasure of being associated with.

When reviewing success factors with your employees, you might also want to go through the company set competencies and how they are performing against these competencies.

Your employees should self-evaluate themselves against the company set competencies ahead of the meeting.

Depending on the number of competencies that your company has listed, you may only discuss competencies that had drastic changes (up or down) from the previous month.

Each individual employee's company set competencies can be monitored, tracked, and updated monthly in a Smartsheet shared document.

Less Talk, More Action

Smartsheet (https://www.smartsheet.com/) is the tool that I have used with my teams in the past to collaborate on shared documents. Smartsheet's motto is "Less Talk, More Action" and has a feel like a Microsoft Excel spreadsheet.

Review Individual Development Plans (IDPs)

Your employees need an opportunity to grow professionally and personally within the safe boundaries of their work environment.

IDPs provide each employee an opportunity to learn new tools and processes or explore other opportunities in the company.

IDPs should not be mandatory because any growth and learning that is not directly connected to their current job performance should be completed outside of work hours (or not recorded as work hours); however, you should take a major interest in helping your employees explore, grow, and challenge themselves professionally.

Managing and running team meetings and one-on-one meetings properly is not only a secret to successfully managing remote teams—it is truly a good practice to develop relationships with your employees that will go beyond your current workplace and into a long-term professional relationship that can span your career.

Every person we meet professionally and personally helps shape who we are and what we leave behind. I pray that each relationship you and I develop is mutually beneficial to each other and helps us all become more caring and compassionate to each other.

[6] http://smallbusiness.chron.com/importance-relationships-workplace-10380.html

Secret Three: Encourage Success

There is more to the success of an employee or a company than just the Key Performance Indicators that lead to success factors. For many companies, these are expectations that are set forth in an employee handbook on certain types of behaviors that are accepted or not accepted.

In addition to these expectations, many companies lay out their core competencies that they use to set expectations and in some cases, to support annual performance reviews.

As a manager, it is your job to search out these company set competencies and to share them with your employees. If your company does not have a set of core competencies written out, I would highly encourage you to recommend that your company move forward with developing one.

In the meantime, you may find the following list of core competencies valuable when getting started with your own employees:

- Adaptability and Flexibility
- Adherence to Company Policy
- Administrative Skills
- Analytical Skills
- Attendance and Punctuality
- Communication - Verbal & Written
- Cost/Expense Management
- Creativity and Innovation
- Culture and Values
- Customer Service Skills
- Efficiency and Effectiveness

- Initiative
- Interpersonal Skills
- Job Knowledge
- Organizational Awareness
- Planning and Organization
- Problem Solving and Decision Making
- Productivity
- Professional Development
- Professionalism
- Quality
- Results and Outcomes
- Self-Management Skills
- Teamwork

Using this list of core competencies, I would ask my remote employees to evaluate themselves against each one using the following scale:

0 - 0.9
Any competencies less than one were areas that were either non-existent or the employee was too new to evaluate themselves against this competency.

If I saw that an employee had rated themselves in this range, it was imperative that I work with them to provide training, guidance, or other support to move up to the next range.

1.0 - 1.9

Any competency that was 1.0 or greater and less than 2.0 was considered an area that the employee did not need to have a strong understanding of or were in the process of growing in their understanding of the competency. An example would be adherence to company policies.

If an employee was an individual contributor and the company they worked for was publicly traded, then they would only need to know the minimum understanding of rules associated with trading stocks and a low number in this competency was acceptable.

However, if the employee was a director or higher in management, then they would need to have a greater understanding of the company policies around trading stocks and this number should be greater.

Again, if the competency had a direct connection to your employee's job or role in the company, your responsibility as their manager is to provide them with training, guidance, or other support to move up to the next stage.

2.0 - 2.9

This range is the range where I expected the majority of my team's competencies to be evaluated. If the employee was strong in Organizational Awareness, but their current position in the company did not require them to be strong in this area, the question I would ask is what other competencies may be getting less attention or suffering because of the time they are spending having a greater awareness of the organization.

If the employee was interested in growing in the company and had an Individual Development Plan that was focused on moving into a role where a greater value in Organization Awareness was a part of the role's job responsibility, then a value greater than 3.0 would be acceptable. However, the time they invested in growing in this competency would need to be on their own personal time over their regular hours.

3.0 - 3.9
This range is the range where the employee would be expected to be in for a small set of competencies that had a strong connection to their role in the company. For example, someone who had a role in public relations would be expected to be in this range for the Communication competency.

If the employee is below this number in a competency that is critical to their success in the role, it could be because of the expectations set based on the role level they are in (a Senior versus a Non-Senior).

As their manager, this is an area where you can help them understand where they should be in this range and create success factors that demonstrate the importance of being successful in this competency for their success in their role.

4.0 - 5.0
Any employee who marks themselves in this range should be questioned to the reasoning behind marking themselves at this level. This is not a request that should force employees to become defensive, but to allow them to articulate their success in this area, which will allow you to support and promote their reasoning behind their rating.

How do I cover all these items in a single meeting?

I'm glad you asked. The first time I go through the company set competencies with an employee, I set aside a longer meeting time to address and explain each competency and the rating scale. Subsequent meetings will only focus on those competencies where they rated themselves very low or very high.

In most cases, monthly self-evaluations by your staff will result in minor differences in individual scores from month to month. However, there will be times where an employee feels they have fallen behind where they need your assistance (training, mentoring, other support, etc.) or where they have excelled in a particular area and they are willing to share examples and reasoning behind their higher number.

In most cases, only about 5 to 10 competencies need to be discussed each month, depending on your employee's self-evaluation scores.

What if I disagree with the rating?

This is where the monthly discussions are invaluable. There will be employees who are not able to articulate why they have rated themselves at such a high number.

You can use that inability to help them either learn to express themselves more effectively or reconsider rating themselves so high. On the other hand, I have had employees rate themselves lower than I would rate them and have helped them see how they are performing better in a particular competency than they might think.

Either way, honest and open discussions are taking place monthly around the core competencies, allowing you to prevent your employees from being surprised at evaluation time by a particular rating you provided to them.

All along you have been having these honest discussions and your employees have a greater understanding of their own strengths and weaknesses.

In the end, the company set competencies will provide you with the tools to help your employees grow professionally and personally.

This focus on their success will allow for difficult discussions to be accepted as an opportunity for them to grow.

This will also have an impact on the team as a whole as each individual understands their strengths and weaknesses in relation to the needs of the team.

Every opportunity we have to evaluate our own strengths and weaknesses and help our employees evaluate theirs will help us become more successful as individuals and as a team.

It is only by self-awareness that we truly understand who we are and represent ourselves with a humble strength that helps our employees grow and find success in their own lives.

Secret Four: Tools

"What a computer is to me is it's the most remarkable tool that we have ever come up with. It's the equivalent of a bicycle for our minds." - Steve Jobs

"All the tools, techniques and technology in the world are nothing without the head, heart, and hands to use them wisely, kindly ,and mindfully." - Rasheed Ogunlaru

Just like a builder of a home, employees who are working remotely must have a set of tools to perform their day-to-day tasks.

As I look at my own toolbox, limited as it is, I see that I have a wide range of tools that I use for different purposes. Now of course, I have duct tape that is the go-to tool for most fixes—effective, but not always the best solution.

Similarly, you will find that you are continually going back to the tool you know (just like the duct tape) to resolve communication and other remote working problems. This tool may be effective but may not be the best solution.

In this chapter, I am going to discuss some of the tools that I have used with my teams throughout the years, and how we used them. By no means are these tools the only tools in their particular market, so I would encourage you to look for the tool in that best fits you, your teams, and your company's needs.

Please note, I have not received any compensation for highlighting these tools. I have listed out the web addresses so that you can make your own decisions.

Microsoft Skype (https://www.skype.com)
Skype is for doing things together. Using Skype's text, voice, video, and screen sharing, you can interact with the people that matter to you, wherever they are. There are two versions of Skype: Personal and Business. I have used both throughout my career.

- **Microsoft Skype for Personal Use**: In my most recent position, we used Skype for Personal Use to minimize the overhead cost of Skype for Business, and we had other tools that were already in place that addressed the missing features in Skype for Business. We would use this tool to support the following:

  o **Divisions' day-to-day conversations**: These conversations consisted of a group that involved multiple teams associated with customer success, consulting, support, and training.

  o **Immediate team's day-to-day discussions**: These discussions consisted of a smaller group of participants that was primarily focused on discussions around training and personal conversations centered only around our team.

  o **Personal conversations**: These were the discussions that were needed between two employees or a small subset of employees to address a specific challenge or simply to keep up with personal challenges and successes that each individual was facing.

- o **One-on-one meetings**: When it was necessary to communicate verbally or visually between two or three employees, we would call each other through Skype. Skype for Personal Use allows you to present yourself visually using your webcam, verbally by using your speakers and microphone (most employees used headsets), share your computer screen, and send files to each other.

  For the most part, we used the verbal communication and the screen sharing. We rarely used video or passed files to each other.

- **Microsoft Skype for Business**: In previous companies, we used Skype for Business that offers the same features as Skype for Personal Use but incorporates into Microsoft's other tools more effectively and contains the following additional features:

  - o Business-related email address and password that spans across multiple Microsoft tools including SharePoint (discussed later)

  - o Advanced call routing that can be used to replace conventional phone systems

  - o Up to 250 users on a single conference call along with multiple conferencing features not available in Skype for Personal Use

  - o Advanced security features to protect your companies' interests

Cisco WebEx (https://www.webex.com/)
WebEx provides a set of tools designed for collaboration no matter where your employees work. It's used to connect a group of individuals, typically through the internet, and allows you to communicate with audio, video, chat, screen sharing, file sharing, and other features.

- **Team meetings**: We used WebEx for team meetings (meetings that usually consisted of more than three people). We were able to perform the majority of actions available to us in Microsoft Skype (verbal and visual communication through the web using a computer audio system, screen sharing, transfer of files, etc.) but on a product that supported a larger number of concurrent users.

- **Meetings with clients**: When it was necessary to meet with clients, we could schedule and invite clients to join us in the WebEx session for training or consulting activities. These sessions could be scheduled ahead of time with a unique WebEx meeting ID that could be passed on to the clients.

- **Group Virtual Instructor Led Training (VILT)**: With WebEx we were also able to schedule group training sessions in advance and open it up for clients to register for the training. One of our instructors would present the training, including slides, demonstrations, and quizzes.

  Depending on the number of clients that registered, we would have a second instructor monitoring the chat window and handling any technical problems.

- **Individual meetings**: There were times when Microsoft Skype or other communication tools were not working properly, and we would switch to using WebEx to run our individual meetings.

Slack (https://slack.com/)
Slack is another communication tool that has a very specific purpose to support teams and streamline communication.

- **Team updates**: For my team, we primarily used Slack for individual updates and explanations of impediments that each individual was facing. In an earlier chapter, I talked about how to run team meetings, and Slack was the tool we would use to list out what was accomplished that day and the impediments we were facing.

  We had a Slack channel that only my team and I had access to and the advantage to this over Skype was that it allowed us to have a historical record that was limited to only updates and impediments that we could easily search and scan through without having side conversations, distracting from the meeting's content.

- **Working with software development**: The software development team had found that Slack was the most effective means to communicate internally among themselves. They allowed us to join particular channels where we could ask questions, share knowledge, and individual conversations.

  Even though Slack is a very powerful tool, I feel that if it was not for software development using it, I would have found another means to enter and track our team updates, eliminating the need to have Slack in my particular team's toolbox.

Toggl (https://www.toggl.com/)[7]
This is a timesheet app for tracking work hours. Use the timer to log task times and get reports based on the time usage. All the time logs are synced to the cloud and you can track time also in the web version, desktop app, Chrome extension and with an Android watch—all your data is safely under one account.

- **Time entry**: Toggl (we used the free version separated based on the overall projects each employee was involved in) allowed my team to track their time using projects. We had particular categories for billable and non-billable time but did not use their billable feature which was only available in the paid product.

  We also used it to track time working on client tasks or meeting with clients. We used tags to identify our clients versus the client's option, which was more effective for paid customers.

  This tool allowed individual team members to track their time by hitting a start and stop button or manually entering in the time. They would also choose a brief description that would allow them and me to distinguish between entries that may be associated with a larger project.

- **Reports**: Toggl allowed me as the manager—who had to provide multiple reports on the overall use of my employees' time—numerous ways to filter and display the data. In addition, I could export the data in a comma separated value (csv) file that was easily imported into Microsoft Excel to perform more granular data compiling.

Email

Yes, email—it is still one of the most effective tools for communication that does not, in my mind, have a viable alternative that is currently available. I guess you could say email is the duct tape and a necessity in everyone's communication toolbox. I won't go into all the ways that we used email, but I will share some tricks.

- **Night owls**: It is a common practice when you move into a management role that you will be tethered to your email and have the strong desire to respond to emails you were not able to get to during the day or emails that come in at night.

  I am not going to tell you that you are wrong doing that, because then I would have to be preaching to myself. (All it takes is a quick search to find numerous studies that discuss the value and problems associated with this connectiveness). What I will say is don't inadvertently force your team members to feel obligated to respond to you if you send emails at night.

  Most email tools have a send delay option that allows you to write your emails at night but not actually send them until the next business day's working hours. This can be an automated process or simply writing your emails and saving them as drafts until the next business day when you can manually send them.

  This is helpful because if you really need your staff to respond to a nighttime email, they will know that if it is important enough for you to send at night, then it must truly be important.

- **Use templates**: Again, most email tools allow for some form of email templates that you can choose when you start writing an email, but if your email software does not have an easy or intuitive way of doing this, simply use Microsoft Notepad (or another simple text editor) to write your drafts and save them to an email template folder.

  You can easily copy and paste the template into your email and fill in the blanks as needed. You will find if you look at the emails you send, there will be some natural templates that you can create from the content you send over and over again.

  In addition, I am going to recommend that you keep your emails short and to the point, but this can come across as bossy and rude if you don't surround these types of emails with general pleasantries.

  A simple template with opening and closing pleasantries can save a large amount of time in the long run.

- **Pick up the phone**: If your email is taking more than five minutes to write, pick up the phone and call the person or set up a meeting to discuss the content of the email you were planning on writing.

  - If you just pick up the phone and call someone, then use the time you would have spent writing out the questions to write a follow-up email describing briefly what you discussed and what action items were agreed upon during the call.

  - If you set up a meeting, put your questions or list of agenda items in the meeting body that you want to address with the person(s) when you meet. This will give them time to think through your questions or have a general idea of what you are going to address. Again, a follow-up email may be useful to provide the action items that were agreed upon in the meeting.

Smartsheet (https://www.smartsheet.com/)
Smartsheet is a web-based project management application that focuses on the collaborative aspects of project management.

- **Project plans**: Smartsheet has some very interesting tools to develop projects and set dependencies on tasks with associated lengths of time to completion along with date assignments. In addition, you can assign individuals to the tasks and have emails automatically sent out to them letting them know which tasks are coming up or which ones are coming due.

There are other numerous features to support projects, but the most useful one is the fact that it is stored in the cloud and accessible by everyone you invite to collaborate on—even at the same time.

- **Smartsheet over Microsoft Excel**: We use both Smartsheet and Microsoft Excel, but I will say that I consider what is the ultimate outcome of the document I am going to create before deciding which tool to use. If it is not heavily dependent on data manipulation or compilation, I pull up Smartsheet and create my document there.

  If it is something that needs multiple individuals (inside my company or outside my company) to collaborate on, I pull up Smartsheet and create my document there.

Data Compiling

Just a note, it is very easy to export your Smartsheet to a Microsoft Excel formatted document to perform data manipulation or compiling. However, because there are so many uses for Smartsheet, I tend to stick with Microsoft Excel from the start for these documents.

Social Media for Business: When you think of social media applications, you might first think of Facebook and pictures of family members across the country. However, social media in itself contains more than just posts on Facebook.

Social media encompasses a wide range of "websites and applications that enable users to create and share content or to participate in social networking"[8]. Businesses small and large are taking advantage of this level of social networking that maintains their company's information (be it documents, videos, audio files, or images).

With 30 plus years in the business world, I have seen numerous of these types of systems, ranging from a simple directory structure on a network to a complete cloud environment that encompasses every part of the business.

The list below provides a quick synopsis of a few that I have used more recently in my career:

- **Alfresco** (https://www.alfresco.com): Alfresco, the name of the product and the company, is a cloud-based Enterprise Content Management (ECM) solution that offers a wide range of document management functionality.[9]

- **Microsoft SharePoint** (https://products.office.com/en-us/sharepoint/sharepoint-server): Microsoft SharePoint is a cloud-based solution that brings together conventionally separate applications, including ECM, social networking, business intelligence, workflow management, personal storage, and web content.[10]

- **Jive** (https://www.jivesoftware.com/): Jive is a social collaboration tool that brings team members, upper management personnel, and other relevant parties in the corporate environment together. It contains numerous features and capabilities to help businesses achieve strategic alignment and improve individual and productivity for employees and teams.[11]

Why can't I find what I am looking for?

Just a note, when you find a file in one of these tools, it is best to locate the link associated with the document and send that link to these individuals. These tools are notorious for being difficult to search.

Salesforce (https://www.salesforce.com/)
It is hard to find any company today that is not using Salesforce for at least a portion of their Customer Relation Management (CRM) software. Salesforce has become the go-to CRM for businesses. However, it is not the only tool and many folks try to turn Salesforce into the duct tape tool to replace all other tools.

Thankfully, you will find many tools (especially many that have already been discussed) that interface with Salesforce to pass data from and to each other.

I have found that the most effective way to use Salesforce in the companies I have worked for is to see it as an internal collaboration tool that spans teams, divisions, and product lines revolving around the client.

If we are looking at ways to have a complete picture of an individual client or an individual company, then there should be tools that either interface with Salesforce or natively have Salesforce built in.

Some examples of how Salesforce has been used in the companies I have worked for include tracking support-related inquiries and outcomes. I've also used it to track sales-related information to include all data associated with the opportunities and outcomes of sales.

In addition, I've used it to provide our clients a community so that they can interact with us and each other regarding our services or products.

There are other tools that we used for completing our day-to-day responsibilities, but the tools I listed in this chapter are revolved around communication with your teams, remote or otherwise. However, as stated in previous chapters, the purpose of tools is to provide a means to improve communication to allow your employees to be the best they can be.

If a tool is cumbersome or impedes the flow of information, then it needs to be evaluated, improved, or replaced. The end goal of tools is people, not just to have a new tool.

[7] https://play.google.com/store/apps/details?id=com.toggl.timer&hl=en
[8] http://www.dictionary.com/browse/social-media
[9] https://reviews.financesonline.com/p/alfresco/
[10] https://reviews.financesonline.com/p/sharepoint/
[11] https://reviews.financesonline.com/p/jive/

Secret Five: Availability

"Don't just be able; always make sure you are available. Be present to make a change." - Israelmore Ayivor

"Your ability will not help if you do not give your availability." - Saji Ijiyemi

I've found that throughout life, where I place my attention is where I find the greatest reward for the effort.

As a manager of remote employees, one of the most important aspects of your job is to actually be there for your team members. This includes having regular meetings as discussed in previous chapters, but also allowing your team members to be free and open to reach out to you when the need arises.

There are exceptions to this as well, but for the most part, providing your team members the freedom to reach out to you when they need your advice is going to reinforce their own ability to come to resolutions on their own as you assist them when their need is greatest.

Making yourself available to your team members will allow them to become more independent and empowered to discover resolutions on their own—one of the great mysteries that seems counterintuitive, but a truth that rings loud in my own life.

I am so busy with management tasks; how do I make myself available?

Redirect your focus.

You were hired to manage a team. Let me say it again, if you have been given the privilege of managing employees, then you have been tasked to lead and direct team members. Okay, one more time.

If you have been asked to manage a group of people (which is the greatest and most costly resource to a company), then you are responsible for actually taking the time to guide, lead, and direct your people.

We need to redirect our thinking that actually leading people is secondary to our positions, and bring our primary focus back to the people performing the tasks.

Doing so will not only make us look good, but make the team look good, the company look good, and can lead to our customers thrilled to work with us.

Here is another counterintuitive secret: The more time you spend guiding, directing, and leading your team members, the less issues you will have to address, giving you more time to guide, direct, and lead your team members.

Alright, what if I am just not available when they reach out?

There are going to be times when you are not available, and you cannot drop everything to meet with your team members. In these circumstances, there are a few ways to address this:

1) In most communication that tools you use to communicate with your staff, you can set your status to Do Not Disturb.

   You will not be notified if any messages come in when in this status. Once you are able to actively accept message again, set yourself back to active status and then review any messages that came in while inactive.

2) If you receive a message when not available (and you had no means to identify to your team members to not disturb you, like possibly a text message), simply respond that you are currently unavailable but will get back to them as soon as you can.

   A simple response allows your team members to know that they are important, but also that you are not able to stop what you are doing at this time to address their needs.

   By acknowledging their request and then following up in a reasonable amount of time, you are providing your team members with tools to address interruptions in their daily activities.

> ### Let me get back with you
> If I am in a meeting when a team member reaches out to me, I will let the meeting guests or organizer know that I have to address a message that came in and will be unable to respond to questions for just a minute while I respond.
>
> This allows me the freedom to respond with a simple "let me get back with you shortly" without worrying I will miss a question being asked of me. In addition, it demonstrates to those I am meeting with the importance that I place on my team members.

What do I do with the messages I received while I was not available for my team members?

If you can address the message, then by all means respond to your team member with your feedback. If you are unable to do so, respond to the messenger letting them know you need additional time to look into it and you will get back to them as soon as possible.

If warranted, you may wish to schedule a meeting with the messenger for later on that day or within a reasonable timeframe.

Is there a way I can be proactive and better manage my team members so that they don't need to reach out to me as often?

The answer to this question is a secret you have already learned: One-on-one meetings. Now before we rehash the advantages of one-on-one meetings, let's address the need for remote employees to have regular interactions with you and others in the company.

This regularity is highly dependent upon the work being done and the personality of your team member, but regardless, you must take an active part in ensuring that your team members have this interaction with you and others for their benefit and your benefit.

Having regular interactions helps build a level of trust necessary for both parties to perform effectively.

Having regular one-on-one meetings allows your employees the opportunity to have a regular meeting time with you. This has been one of the most effective ways that I have been able to minimize the times that my team members need to reach out to me.

If there is a non-emergency question that comes up between these one-on-one meetings, my team members have kept a log of the questions and wait until our one-on-one meeting to ask them.

One-on-one meetings are really for your team members, not for you, this is a perfect opportunity for the team members to ask these questions knowing that you have set aside this time just for them.

Help your team members help themselves and others.
Years ago, I worked with a senior application engineer that told me and other new application engineers that he would answer any question once, and only once. If we did not remember or write down the answer that he provided, then it was on us that we did not find a way to remember the answer, not on him to keep answering the same question over and over again.

I tested him multiple times on this, and true to his word, he would remember that I asked that same question and would just give me that look. I knew I was busted and walked away shocked at his memory.

Needless to say, this story, although not my style, makes a point—we need to help our team members find ways to answer questions themselves in the future. In addition, we need to help our team members help others learn from their knowledge as well.

If there are questions or situations that come up during our one-on-one's that I feel would be beneficial to the other team members, or even other teams, I will ask the team member to write an email, a blog post, a knowledge article (usually associated with Online Communities), or possibly even a quick training that we can pass on to others.

It is very common that if one individual has a question, then there are others that have the same question or may not even be aware that they had the same question.

Having your team members take a positive role in helping others learn will help highlight their skills and provide greater insight into your team's abilities.

Your responsibility as the manager of the team is to highlight your team's accomplishments in public and address your team members' areas for improvement in private.

LinkedIn (https://www.linkedin.com)
LinkedIn is a business- and employment-oriented social networking service that operates via websites and mobile apps. It has become the primary place where individuals highlight their business-related and volunteer accomplishments, and it is a great place to help your team members highlight their own business accomplishments.

I have regularly recommended my team members to post, like, and interact with LinkedIn to highlight themselves and our company. It is a great way to help your employees see that you are interested in their career long-term, not just for the time they are working with you and your company.

Secret Six: Instill Trust

"The best way to find out if you can trust somebody is to trust them." - Ernest Hemingway

"Trust is the glue of life. It's the most essential ingredient in effective communication. It's the foundational principle that holds all relationships." - Stephen R. Covey

It is universal that one of the greatest challenges we face is to grant our trust to individuals without them first proving that our trust is warranted.

This also is one of the biggest failures that we can make as a manager of remote teams, especially new managers or new team members.

Trust is truly the means by which we are able to move forward with communication that produces results.

What does it look like when team members do not trust each other?

I believe that each of us has been in a situation where there is a lack of trust between parties; either it be in your personal life or your business life. The following is a sample of the results when there is a lack of trust between parties:

- **What do they really mean?** Questioning the meaning behind each statement that is presented. This negates effective communication because it makes the receiving party spend more time determining the hidden meaning behind a statement, versus taking the statement as face value and moving forward with the actions that may be associated with the statement.

- **Theft**: Not trusting the presenter of information results in wasted time which really is stealing from the time that we are being paid to work. It also is stealing the energy we could be applying to moving forward with the actions that may be associated with the statement presented.

- **Morale killer**: Finally, not trusting can become an infectious weed that penetrates a team and destroys morale. Without trust, team members can default to bringing in others to determine the meaning behind statements and can infect others that are being drawn into the conversations.

How can I instill trust with my team, especially when I am new or a team member is new?

Ask them for their trust. My motto when I am put into a position to manage a new team or a new team member is to ask them to trust me now, with the goal that the trust they place in me will be warranted in the future—hopefully near future.

Your job as a manager is to provide your teams with a safe environment where they can trust you and then to live up to that trust.

Your team inherently wants to trust you; taking the time to ask them for that trust goes a long way in instilling trust with your team members.

Ask them to trust each other. The goal is not only for them to trust you, but to trust their fellow team members as well. You must help your team move past the thinking that others on the team are trying to make them look bad, or that they should make themselves look good at the expense of their teammates.

This may take time, but by asking them to trust each other, you are on the first step to improving communication and moving forward with team effectiveness.

Now that I have asked them to trust me and their team members, how can I ensure that trust is maintained?

Team meetings

We have discussed team meetings in a previous chapter, but I want to reiterate some of the key points to running a team meeting that instills trust.

- **Team building, five minutes at a time**: The first five minutes of your meeting should be a time for water cooler talk where the team gets to learn about each other's lives. Teams that are invested in each other personally are more likely to trust each other.

  Providing the time for the remote team members to shoot the breeze at the beginning of your team meetings will pay numerous dividends in productivity of individual team members and the team as a whole.

- **Keep it positive**: Team meetings should be focused on the items we can control as a team. If there is a need to address the tasks of our fellow team members or another team, it is our responsibility as managers to ensure that those conversations remain positive.

  If there are concerns between team members, or between other teams, we must ask our team members to hold off discussing it further in the group meeting and hold their concerns until our one-on-one meeting or another scheduled meeting where we can talk about their concerns in private.

- **Provide each team member the ability to demonstrate their expertise**: Providing your individual team members with the ability to present a topic or to share an experience that they learned takeaways from will go a long way with other team members seeing them as teammates that bring expertise with them.

- **Everyone has a birthday**: Use the birthday method (reference Secret Two) to ensure that everyone on the team has a chance to share their impediments and to speak to the entire team. Again, providing everyone a safe place to share their thoughts is a necessity to instilling trust among the team.

One-on-one meetings
We have discussed one-on-one meetings in a previous chapter as well, but again, reiterating the key points to running a one-on-one meeting will help you see how you can use these meeting to instill trust.

- **I am all ears**: This is your team member's meeting with you, it is not your meeting to meet with them. You should be *all ears* to help your team members address their needs. Listen actively and respond with steps you will do or need to do to help them be successful in their roles.

- **Manager/Team Member confidentiality**: Your team members should be comfortable to talk to you about their struggles. One-on-one meetings do not have to necessarily be positive, your team members need the opportunity to express their concerns with you openly and honestly.

- This requires a level of agreed upon confidentiality. What they share in our one-on-one meetings is kept between us unless what they share is going to hurt them, the company, or a client.

- **Help them practice**: There will be times when you will ask your team members to bring up their concerns in a public setting. Your job is to help them come up with the way to bring up their concerns that will allow the recipient of their concerns feel that they are working together to help each other, not trying to make the recipient look bad.

  You may even ask your team members to role play how they are going to bring up their concerns with a fellow team member or another team.

Running meetings effectively will help your team members see you as someone they can trust and ensure that communication is not hindered by a lack of trust. You can have no greater achievement in life than to have others say that they trust your words and your actions.

Secret Seven: Managing Beyond

"The purpose of life is not to be happy. It is to be useful, to be honorable, to be compassionate, to have it make some difference that you have lived and lived well." - Ralph Waldo Emerson

"Successful people are always looking for opportunities to help others. Unsuccessful people are always asking, 'What's in it for me?'" - Brian Tracy

Are you ready for the last secret to managing remote employees?

This secret, which could seem counterintuitive, is the secret that puts all the secrets in the proper light—life is not about you.

It does not matter if you are leading a few individuals or thousands of individuals, it does not matter if you are an individual contributor or the chief executive officer of an organization, nothing matters if we are focused on serving ourselves versus serving others.

Your job as a leader, regardless if you are managing remote employees or not, is to serve your team.

You have to manage beyond yourself and put your team members first in the day-to-day responsibilities of the role in which you serve.

How do I manage beyond myself?

Manage beyond your company

The first way you manage beyond yourself is by managing beyond the confines of your company. In this day and age, it is unlikely that the team members you are managing now will be with your company in the next few years.

This is not a bad thing, this is just the truth that for talented folks, there will always be other opportunities and circumstances in their lives will inevitably change. Folks that leave your company leave for many reasons, but I can say that if you follow these rules, the likelihood they will leave because of your leadership is unlikely.

Managing your employees for their long-term careers produces the following results:

- **Honest discussions on performance**: For most managers, the need to talk to their team members about negative performance is a chore and produces a level of anxiety that is usually felt by both parties. However, when you are managing beyond your company, you have the freedom to discuss performance issues in a positive light.

  Your role is helping your team members grow in an area that they may not even realize they are not performing well in. Your role is to coach them for improvement for long-term success in their careers, not just the role they are currently filling in your company.

If the performance change does not take place as required, your role is to help them move on to a role that better fits their skill sets. This can be with your company or having to let them go to find a position with another company that will be a better fit for them. In this light, you are actually helping your team members find long-term success.

- **Wanting to stay:** It is extremely likely that your employees will find great success under your leadership if you follow the secrets in this book. Good leaders are like good neighbors— you have to think twice before leaving, knowing that the likelihood of finding good leaders (or neighbors) is relatively small.

Even though it is my hope that a new generation of leaders will be raised up as more and more individuals are led by managers that follow these secrets, or just as important, you the reader follow these secrets, it is very unlikely that most leaders are actually following all of these secrets.

For your team members who have had been led by leaders who do not see themselves as servants to their teams, your leadership is going to be most welcome.

This will inevitably lead to great job satisfaction with your team members and reduce turnover. And any HR representative will tell you, turnover is costly and has a short-term and long-term effect on the entire organization.

Manage beyond the day-to-day tasks
Your role as a leader is to develop an enthusiasm for your team members, not the individual tasks. This is going to force you to step away from the day-to-day tasks and force the majority of your energy to be spent on getting to know your team members.

While your team members have to be the experts in the tasks, you need to become the expert in your team members.

Your role is now to serve their needs to help them be the most productive they can be.

Manage beyond your own dreams
We all have dreams that we hope to achieve in life. Many of these dreams are tied up in our professional success.

Dreams, as good as they may be, are only truly good if they go beyond our own happiness and success.

Dreams that are centered around helping others have long-term staying power and a greater impact on society as a whole.

Helping others achieve their dreams

My dreams are centered on helping others be the best they can be in the position in which they serve. For me, this means, that my dreams are linked with the dreams of others and them finding success in their dreams.

You may have different dreams that have a similar outcome, and if that is so, I wish you all the best. However, even if your dreams are more self-focused, you will find that helping others achieve their dreams has a positive effect in you achieving your own dreams.

Conclusion

Now that you have learned about me and the secrets to managing a remote team, you may be feeling a little overwhelmed with all that it will take to put these secrets into practice.

I want to encourage you to make a decision to do one step today, then do another step a month from now, and another step a month later, and so on until you have truly put into practice all of these secrets.

You will find that you will gain time back from putting these secrets into practice and less than a year from now your team will be the envy of all the teams in your organization, and you will be one of the reasons that your team members love to come to work every day.

Tell them, teach them, remind them
As an educator, I find the best training involves the following three steps: Tell them what you are going to teach them, teach them what you told them you were going to teach them, and remind them of what you taught them.

Putting that practice in to the end of this book brings us back to the acronym *PRETAIM*:

- **Purpose**: Provide a common purpose to rally your team around.

- **Relationships**: Develop and encourage positive working relationships through communication with your team members and among your team members.

- **Encourage success**: Develop a means to help your team be successful beyond just the tasks they have been assigned to complete.

- **Tools**: Provide and use the best tools to allow your teams to be successful.

- **Availability**: Make yourself available to your team.

- **Instill trust**: Ask your team to trust you and then live up to that trust.

- **Manage beyond**: Focus on serving your team, not yourself.

It is my hope that you will put these secrets into practice and find success in helping your team members find their success.

Appendix: Additional Thoughts

The following information is one of many additional thoughts that I wanted to share in this book but never found a chapter to put this into that did not distract from the secret being shared.

Letting team members go

I have had to perform multiple reduction in force (RIF) and performance related layoffs in my career. I have been trained by numerous Human Resources managers on how to perform these layoffs to ensure that the company is protected and have had these same steps applied to my own RIF layoff.

Before I discuss ways to manage beyond layoffs, please check with your HR department first on the acceptability of these steps.

To manage beyond a RIF or performance-related layoff, consider the following steps:

- Write up a recommendation highlighting the skill sets that you can honestly say that they performed well in. This can be a letter they can show to a prospective employer, or a recommendation on LinkedIn (https://www.linkedin.com).

- Take the time to reach out in your own network to help them find a position that will better meet their skill set.

- Reach out to them every few weeks to see how they are doing—this may involve simply an email or a phone call. Either way, ask them if there is anything you can do to assist them. Sometimes this leads back to those conversations where you can help them grow professionally to help their long-term career.

Why should I do this even if my HR department says it is OK to do?

I will tell you that this has been one of the greatest joys in my life, helping others in what could be seen as the worst thing that has ever happened to them. Also, you may find yourself in the same position one day and having a track record of helping others during this time in their lives will pay big dividends in your own life—remember that reaping what you sow works beyond just the fields.

Made in the USA
Monee, IL
02 June 2020